Eman Schools
11965 Allisonville Rd.
Fishers, IN 46038

DISCOVERING

GERMANY

EMAN SCHOOL LIBRARY

By Philip Steele

CRESTWOOD HOUSE
New York

A ZOË BOOK

© 1993 Zoë Books Limited

First American publication 1993 by Crestwood House, Macmillan Publishing Company, 866 Third Avenue, New York, NY 10022

Macmillan Publishing Company is part of the Maxwell Communication Group of Companies

First published in Great Britain in 1993 by Zoë Books Limited, 15 Worthy Lane, Winchester, Hampshire SO23 7AB

Devised and produced by
Zoë Books Limited
15 Worthy Lane
Winchester
Hampshire SO23 7AB

All rights reserved. No part of this book may be reproduced or transmitted in any form or by any means, electronic or mechanical, including photocopying, recording, or by any information storage and retrieval system, without the prior permission in writing from the Publisher.

Printed in Italy by Grafedit SpA
Design: Jan Sterling, Sterling Associates
Picture research: Suzanne Williams
Map: Gecko Limited
Production: Grahame Griffiths

8 7 6 5 4 3 2 1

Library of Congress Cataloging-in-Publication Data

Steele, Philip, 1948-
  Germany / by Philip Steele.
    p. cm. — (Discovering)
  Includes index.
  Summary: Introduces the geography, people, everyday life, history, and politics of Germany.
  ISBN 0-89686-777-3
  1. Germany — Juvenile literature. [1. Germany.]
I. Title. II. Series.
DD17.S68 1993
943 — dc20   92-39685

Photographic acknowledgments
The publishers wish to acknowledge, with thanks, the following photographic sources:

Cover and title page: Zefa; 5 Robert Harding Picture Library; 6, 7l Zefa; 7r Robert Harding Picture Library; 8 Zefa; 9l Robert Harding Picture Library; 9r, 10 Zefa; 11l Staatsarchiv, Hamburg/ Bridgeman Art Library; 11r Zefa; 12 Frank Spooner Pictures; 13l Robert Harding Picture Library; 13r: detail from the cathedral scene from *Faust*, "Margaret tormented by the evil spirits," by Frank Cadogan Cowper, Private Collection/ Bridgeman Art Library; 14 Zefa; 15, 16 Robert Harding Picture Library; 17l Zefa; 17r, 18 Robert Harding Picture Library; 19l, 19r Zefa; 20, 21, 22 Robert Harding Picture Library; 23, 24 Zefa; 25 Musée Condé Chantilly, Giraudon/Bridgeman Art Library; 26 Neil Bruce Photographic; 27l, 27r Rex Features; 28 Frank Spooner Pictures; 29l Rex Features; 29r Frank Spooner Pictures.

Cover: *Main Square, Bremen*

Title page: *View of the town of Berchtesgaden, in Bavaria*

Contents

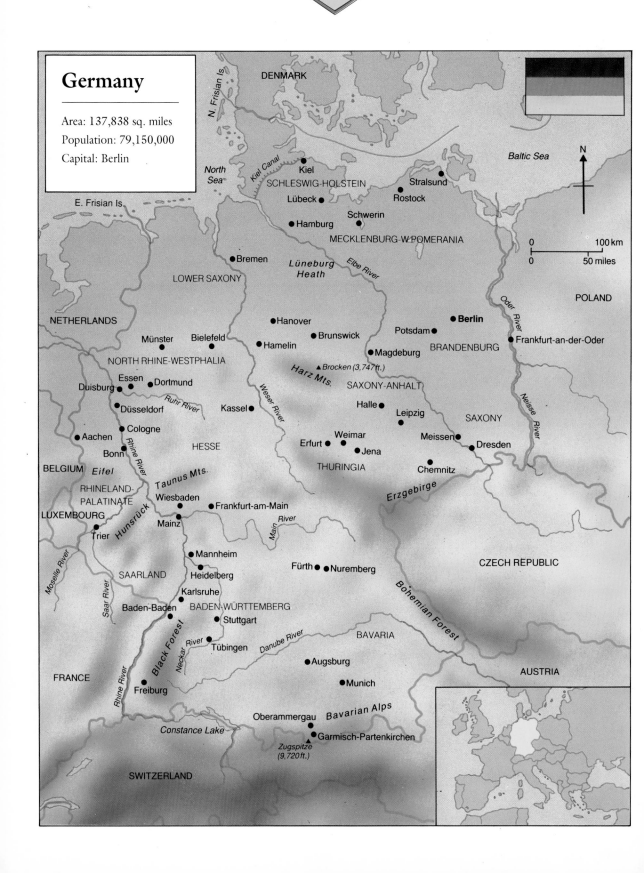

Germany

Area: 137,838 sq. miles
Population: 79,150,000
Capital: Berlin

DENMARK

N. Frisian Is.

North Sea

Baltic Sea

Kiel Canal

Kiel

SCHLESWIG-HOLSTEIN

Lübeck

Stralsund

Rostock

Schwerin

E. Frisian Is.

Hamburg

MECKLENBURG-W. POMERANIA

N

Bremen

Lüneburg Heath

Elbe River

LOWER SAXONY

POLAND

0   100 km
0   50 miles

NETHERLANDS

Münster

Bielefeld

Hanover

Brunswick

Potsdam

Berlin

Oder River

Frankfurt-an-der-Oder

Hamelin

Magdeburg

BRANDENBURG

NORTH RHINE-WESTPHALIA

Weser River

Brocken (3,747 ft.)

Harz Mts.

SAXONY-ANHALT

Essen

Dortmund

Ruhr River

Kassel

Halle

Leipzig

SAXONY

Neisse River

Duisburg

Düsseldorf

Cologne

HESSE

Erfurt

Weimar

Jena

Meissen

Dresden

Aachen

Rhine River

Bonn

THURINGIA

Chemnitz

BELGIUM

Eifel

Taunus Mts.

RHINELAND-PALATINATE

Wiesbaden

Erzgebirge

LUXEMBOURG

Hunsrück

Mainz

Frankfurt-am-Main

Main River

Trier

Moselle River

Saar River

Mannheim

Fürth

Nuremberg

CZECH REPUBLIC

SAARLAND

Heidelberg

Karlsruhe

Baden-Baden

BADEN-WÜRTTEMBERG

Black Forest

Neckar River

Stuttgart

BAVARIA

Bohemian Forest

Tübingen

Danube River

Augsburg

AUSTRIA

FRANCE

Freiburg

Munich

Rhine River

Oberammergau

Bavarian Alps

Constance Lake

Garmisch-Partenkirchen

Zugspitze (9,720 ft.)

SWITZERLAND

Willkommen!

Welcome to Germany! This large country lies at the heart of northern Europe. It stretches from the gray waves of the North Sea and Baltic coasts to the snowy peaks of the Bavarian Alps in the south. In the west, the Moselle River winds through sunny vineyards. To the east lie the vast plains and the forests of Poland.

The northern coasts and lowlands have a fairly mild climate. Farther south, winter in the uplands and mountains is longer and harsher — but the summers are often much hotter.

About 200 years ago, Germany was a patchwork of small countries, states and independent cities. Between 1945 and 1990 Germany was divided into the Federal Republic of Germany (FRG) and the German Democratic Republic (GDR). Today it is a single nation.

The Berlin Wall symbolized the division of Germany. In 1989 many people joined in to help knock it down.

One federation

Although Germany is now one country, there are still many differences among the regions. The country is divided into states, called *Länder*. The *Länder* are able to make many of their own laws, but they also join together under a central government. This is called a federal system of government.

The German language is spoken by everyone. However, there are great differences in local dialects depending on the region. The Swabian and Bavarian dialects are widespread in the south, while in the north Low German, which has much in common with English, is spoken.

At school, children learn the standard version of the language — *Hochdeutsch*, or High German. This is the language of business and of newspapers and television.

Germany in Europe

Since the 1960s many people from other European countries have come to live and work in Germany. They are from Eastern Europe, the former Yugoslavia, Turkey, Italy and Greece.

Germany is a leading member of the European Community (EC). It has close ties with France, Britain and other EC members. In recent years Germany has also developed new trading links with its neighbors to the east.

Along the Rhine

To many people the idea of typical German scenery is a broad, winding river passing between steep banks covered in vineyards and pretty villages. Castles perch on the tops of hills. This is typical of parts of the 823-mile-long Rhine River. It forms Germany's border with Switzerland and the Alsace region of France, before flowing northward through Germany and the Netherlands to the North Sea. There are many stories about the Rhine. Perhaps the most famous is the legend of the Lorelei, a maiden whose beautiful voice was said to lure sailors onto rocks in the middle of the river.

The Rhine valley is an ancient trading route. The river is still busy with barges today. It takes about eight days to carry cargo from Basel in Switzerland to the Dutch port of Rotterdam. This excellent waterway encouraged many large industrial cities to grow up along the Rhine. The waste from their factories has polluted its waters.

Borderlands

Germany's western border is a meeting place with French language and traditions. In the past, Saarland, a region of coal and steel production, was part of France. Its chief river, the Saar, flows into the Moselle to the southwest of Trier.

To the north of the Moselle, the land rises to the Eifel plateau, where the picturesque villages look very like those across the border in Belgium and Luxembourg. To the southeast of the Moselle lies the farmland of the Hunsrück. This is part of the *Land* of Rhineland-Palatinate, whose capital is at Mainz, where the Rhine meets the Main River.

Pfalz, an old customs post on the Rhine

From 1945 to 1990, it was the capital of the Federal Republic of Germany. Bonn is a quiet university town, where the great musical composer Ludwig van Beethoven was born in 1770. From there the Rhine flows north to Cologne, famed for its twin-spired cathedral, and Düsseldorf, a center of business, arts and entertainment. Each year, before the Christian season of Lent, carnival is celebrated in the region. There are crazy processions and merrymaking. This region also boasts the world's largest inland port at Duisburg, where the Ruhr River joins the Rhine. From the 1850s onward the Ruhr area became one of Europe's most industrialized regions, with coal mines, steel mills and smoking factory chimneys. Busy cities grew up at Essen and Dortmund. Today's factories are quieter·and cleaner, but pollution remains a problem.

Cologne Cathedral

Zum Wohl! — Your good health!

It is said that the ancient Romans first planted grapevines along the valley of the Rhine. Today German wines are known all over the world. Most are white wines, made from famous grape varieties such as *Riesling*. Red wines are also produced. When the vines are harvested in September, festivals are held in many of the Rhineland's farming villages.

Fun and factories

Farther north along the Rhine is the *Land* of North Rhine-Westphalia, where beer rather than wine is brewed. In the south of the *Land* is the city of Bonn.

Forests and mountains

Summer days in the Black Forest, or *Schwarzwald*, are best spent hiking or youth hosteling. Germany's southwest corner is a region of wooded hills, old farmhouses and peaceful meadows. Among the dark firs of the forests, there are clearings filled with wildflowers.

The cathedral city of Freiburg-im-Breisgau still has fine buildings dating back to the Middle Ages. The Black Forest and its towns are in the *Land* of Baden-Württemberg. This region is crossed by the Neckar River, which joins the Rhine at Mannheim.

On the banks of the Neckar are the romantic old university towns of Heidelberg and Tübingen, as well as the prosperous industrial city of Stuttgart surrounded by vineyards and rolling green countryside. Baden-Württemberg produces electrical goods and the famous Mercedes-Benz and Porsche cars.

To the south, on the Swiss border, is Lake Constance, or *Bodensee*. To the east lies the *Land* of Bavaria, which borders Austria and Czechoslovakia. Bavaria has many beautiful old towns, such as Nuremberg, which has been famous since the Middle Ages for its Christmas fair, its gingerbread and its toy making. Its lively capital is Munich, a center for industry and the arts.

Farmhouses in the Black Forest

Skiing is popular in southern Germany.

Visiting the Alps

The high peaks of the Bavarian Alps can be seen from the center of Munich. They reach their highest point at the Zugspitze, which is 9,720 feet above sea level. Visitors to its summit can see as far as the Bohemian Forest on the Czech border, 100 miles away. Winter snows attract many visitors to ski resorts such as Garmisch-Partenkirchen.

Alpine farmhouses are built of wood, with sloping roofs. Many are beautifully carved or painted. Each summer, villagers lead their herds of dairy cows up to graze the high pastures.

Oberammergau, a village in southern Bavaria, has become famous for its Passion play, which is held every ten years. The play retells the story of the crucifixion and resurrection of Jesus, with local people taking all the parts. The play was first performed in 1634, to mark the end of a terrible plague.

Fairy-tale castles

Ludwig II ruled Bavaria from 1864 until 1886, when he was declared mad. Ludwig was not a good ruler, but he loved the music of Richard Wagner and romantic tales from the Middle Ages. He spent vast sums of money building dreamlike castles amid the mountains and lakes of Bavaria. Neuschwanstein Castle is the most famous of these.

The center and north

The Frankfurt skyline across the Main River

Frankfurt-am-Main is famous for its many trade fairs. The city is a center of banking and insurance and home of the German stock exchange. It has one of Europe's busiest airports. Germany's national airline, Lufthansa, carries businesspeople to Frankfurt from around the world.

Frankfurt is the largest city in the *Land* of Hesse, but the regional capital is at Wiesbaden, in the wooded foothills of the Taunus region.

In the north of Hesse is the industrial city of Kassel. Here, exhibits in a museum tell the story of the brothers Jacob and Wilhelm Grimm. In the 1800s few people could read and most stories were told. The two brothers traveled around Hesse and wrote down many of the folktales that they heard. Today these stories — one of which is *Little Red Riding Hood* —

are known all over the world.

Another famous German folktale is based on the town of Hamelin. It dates back to the year 1284, when, it was said, a pied piper charmed away the town's rats, drowning them in the Weser River. When the mayor refused to pay the piper, he charmed away the children of the town. They were never seen again.

Hamelin is in the *Land* of Lower Saxony, which stretches westward to the Dutch border. This is a region of peat bogs, moors and heathland. The Lüneburg Heath, with its purple heather, is a good place to go horseback riding. Most of the *Land* is given over to farming and forestry.

The regional capital of Lower Saxony is Hanover. This city has close historical ties with Britain. In 1714 the German-speaking ruler of Hanover became King George I of Great Britain and Ireland.

Independent cities

During the Middle Ages, German merchants set up a trading network called the Hanseatic league. This became very wealthy, with warehouses from London to Moscow. Hanseatic cities became powerful and ran their own affairs.

Many of these cities are still great trading centers today. The North Sea ports of Hamburg, on the Elbe River, and Bremen, on the Weser River, are *Länder* in their own right. Today they rely on the aviation industry and electronics as well as shipping. However, the houses of the old merchant families and sea captains may still be seen.

This old manuscript shows the port of Hamburg, when the Hanseatic league was powerful.

When it is not so sunny, these wicker seats are sometimes used as wind shelters.

Looking north

Vacationers come to Germany's northern coasts for the sailing, the beaches and the bird watching. Offshore, the North and East Friesian islands include tourist resorts such as Sylt and Norderney. The Friesian people, whose territory stretches westward into the Netherlands, have their own traditions and language.

Germany's most northern *Land* is called Schleswig-Holstein. It forms a narrow strip of land between the North Sea and the Baltic Sea, which are linked by the Kiel Canal (known in German as the *Nord-Ostsee Kanal*). More than 62 miles long, this is the busiest canal in the world.

The green farmland of the region was for many years claimed by both Germany and Denmark. This long dispute was finally settled in 1920. Farming, fishing and trade provide work, and there are large ports at Kiel and at Lübeck, one of the most beautiful of the old Hanseatic cities.

Eastern Germany

Eastern Germany stretches from the dunes and cliffs of the Baltic coast southward to the Erzgebirge, a range of hills on the border with Czechoslovakia. The Elbe River flows from here across eastern Germany to Hamburg. The eastern border with Poland is marked by the Oder and Neisse rivers.

During the 1930s Germany was ruled by a racist political party called the Nazis. They wanted to conquer all of Europe but were defeated in 1945. Germany was then divided into two. For almost half of this century, eastern Germany formed a separate country, the German Democratic Republic (GDR).

The GDR was a communist state, with state-owned factories and farms. The government followed the ideas of Karl Marx, the political thinker who was born at Trier in 1818.

Today the east has once again joined up with the western part of Germany. Eastern Germany has been divided into five new *Länder*. There have been many changes. Whereas the state used to own industry, it is now run in the capitalist way with privately owned businesses. The east now faces a number of problems, including unemployment, social unrest and heavy industrial pollution in its cities.

This power station is south of Leipzig, in the former GDR.

Cities of the east

Although Schwerin is the regional capital of Mecklenburg, the *Land*'s largest city is the Hanseatic port of Rostock. This was the former GDR's biggest port and a center of shipbuilding. A smaller Hanseatic port, Stralsund, lies to the east.

Eastern Germany's heavy industry is found farther south, around the cities of Magdeburg, Halle, Leipzig, Chemnitz and Dresden. Jena, home of the Zeiss company, has long been known for its quality lenses, cameras and microscopes. Meissen has been famous since 1710 as the home of German porcelain, or fine china.

Until World War II (1939–1945), Dresden was one of the world's most beautiful cities. It was destroyed by bombs during the worst air raid ever experienced in Europe. After 1945 the government of the GDR carefully rebuilt or restored many of Dresden's finest old buildings.

Dresden castle was built between 1530 and 1701.

This detail from a painting by F. C. Cowper shows a scene from Faust. *One of the characters is being tormented by an evil spirit.*

Faust and the witches

The Harz Mountains lie across the former border between the FRG and the GDR. Here, among the wooded hills, are pretty villages dating back to the Middle Ages. The highest peak of the region is the Brocken, at 3,746 feet.

It is said that witches come here to dance on Mayday Eve. This scene is shown in *Faust*, a play by Germany's most famous writer, Johann Wolfgang von Goethe. Goethe was a brilliant poet, scientist and thinker, who was born at Frankfurt-am-Main in 1749. In 1776 he settled at the court of the duke of Weimar, near Erfurt.

Berlin

The Brandenburg Gate is at the center of Berlin.

Germany's capital, Berlin, is overlooked by the massive Brandenburg Gate, with its huge stone columns and horse-drawn chariot of copper. Berlin is a large, sprawling city of three million inhabitants. It has an area of 339 square miles. Berlin became important in the early 1700s, as capital of the powerful state of Prussia. In 1871 the separate states of Germany were united, and Berlin was declared the capital. It became a center of industry and learning.

By the 1920s Berlin was a fashionable center of experimental art, drama, film and jazz. The city was famous for its bars and cafés, and its sharp humor. In the 1930s it was also the scene of political troubles, with violent clashes between the Communists and the members of the Nazi party. When the Nazis finally came to power in Germany, they waged war with the rest of Europe. By their defeat in 1945, Berlin had been bombed into rubble.

A divided city

After World War II, Berlin, like the rest of Germany, was divided. East Berlin, occupied by the Soviet Union's Red Army, became capital of the communist GDR. West Berlin, occupied by the troops of Britain, France and the United States, found itself surrounded on all sides by the new GDR. It depended for survival on the capitalist countries on the west and the FRG, for the United States and the Soviet Union were now bitter enemies. Berlin was at the center of worldwide tension in a period known as the political cold war.

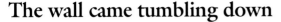

The wall came tumbling down

In 1961 the GDR ordered the division of Berlin by a wall across the city. No one was allowed to leave East Berlin to go to the west. Many people tried to cross the wall illegally, but they were shot. Not until 1989 did the Berlin Wall come down. Berliners celebrated as their city at last became one again.

Sights to see

The Tiergarten – Berlin's largest park surrounds the *Siegessäule*, a 219-foot-high column with 285 steps to the top. The park stretches from the Brandenburg Gate to Berlin's famous zoo.

The Memorial Church – One of the most famous city landmarks is a ruined tower. It was the only part of the famous *Gedächtniskirche* to survive wartime bombing.

Charlottenburg – This beautiful royal palace dates back to 1695. Set in formal gardens, it houses fine paintings and tapestries.

Museums and galleries – The western suburb of Dahlem is home to fine art galleries, botanical gardens and a series of exciting museums. The east of the city also houses ancient treasures, in the world-famous Pergamon Museum and in the National Gallery.

A city for youth

Berlin's districts are linked by an underground railway, or *U-bahn*. At the center of the city are large stores, high-rise offices, hotels and famous street cafés.

Berlin's two most famous streets are the *Kurfürstendamm* (known to all as the *Ku'damm*) and *Unter den Linden*. Berlin is a world center of opera, classical music and theater.

Districts such as Kreuzberg attract the young people of Berlin. Today's city is, as ever, a center of political protest, of outrageous fashion, of art and experimental theater, of bands and nightclubs.

Many of Berlin's outer suburbs, in both east and west, are made up of tall apartment buildings. On summer weekends Berliners like to escape to the many lakes, rivers and woods that surround the city to cycle, walk, swim, windsurf or just sunbathe.

The bright lights of the Ku'damm

People at work

Germany is now Europe's leading industrial power. Germany's plains and hills contain many minerals used in industry. Metal ores are mined in Lower Saxony and Thuringia. Germany has some oil and large fields of coal and lignite (a brown, woody form of coal). These fuels are used to generate power. Nuclear and hydroelectric power also provide electricity for industry and homes.

Heavy industries such as mining, iron and steel are still important, but Germany has become better known for its manufacture of cars and trucks, its textiles, electronics and chemicals. Names such as Volkswagen, BMW, Siemens, Braun, Bosch, Hoechst and Bayer have become famous around the world.

German firms have a reputation for good training, hard work and efficiency. More Germans now work in services than in manufacturing. They go to work in offices, banks and supermarkets rather than in mines or factories.

In the old days, German women were expected to limit their activities to *Kirche, Küche und Kinder* (church, kitchen and children). Today women play a leading part in industry, business and politics. They make up about 39 percent of the work force. In the eastern *Länder*, however, political changes since 1990 have not favored women. There, they now make up nearly two-thirds of the unemployed.

The rights of working people are protected by trade unions. Many workers have a say in how their firms are run.

Germany's car factories are among the most advanced in the world.

Haymaking in the Bavarian Alps

Working in the countryside

As in other European countries, machines now do much of the work once done by farm workers. Only a small proportion of Germans still work on the land, but large crops of wheat, barley, potatoes and sugar beets are produced.

Beef and dairy cattle, sheep and chickens are raised. Pigs provide pork for sausages and other traditional dishes. Many farms are still small and family owned. All members of the family may lend a hand with the farm work. Sometimes they combine this with working in the nearest town.

Southern Germany still has large areas of pine forest and exports timber. In recent years foresters have become worried by the damage to trees caused by acid rain. This falls when the air becomes polluted by factory smoke and exhaust fumes from cars.

Fishing

Fishery on Germany's northern coasts has also been affected by a changing world. The European Community has had to place strict limits on the size of catches because there are fewer herring than in the old days.

Stores and markets

As in other parts of Europe, Germans do more and more of their shopping at large, suburban supermarkets. In the city centers there are large department stores as well as corner stores and street markets. Many cities have traditional Christmas markets that have been in business for hundreds of years.

A street market at Tübingen

Everyday life

For German children, the day begins early. School starts at 8 A.M. but finishes by 1 P.M. when most children go home for lunch. There are no school uniforms, and children wear casual clothes to school. Younger children have the afternoon free, once they have done their homework. Older children may return to school in the early afternoon for special study or activity groups. In the summer children often go to the swimming pools in the afternoon. In the winter they may go skating.

In the afternoons and evenings and during school holidays, many children go to their local teen clubs to meet up with their friends. The clubs may have their own cafés and may sponsor indoor games and sports. There may be dances or amateur rock concerts as well.

As in other northern European countries, people like to head for the sunshine during their summer vacations. Many Germans travel each year to Spain, Greece or the south of France.

These German children are learning to speak English in a school language laboratory.

Cities and suburbs

Eight out of ten Germans live in towns and cities. Many live in apartments or in houses with small gardens. Large suburbs were built around many German cities during the 1950s and 1960s. The developments often include playgrounds for young children and centers for teen clubs and community meetings.

Trains and buses link the suburbs with the city centers. Modern streetcars are used in many cities, and their lines often connect with an underground network. However, the family car is as popular as ever, despite increasing traffic jams and crowded highways, or *Autobahnen*.

Many cities are ringed by green areas where people can relax and enjoy fresh air. Here you can see joggers keeping fit. On the weekends the parks may be busy with groups of foreign workers getting together or with family groups cycling along traffic-free paths.

Germans have a reputation for enjoying fitness activities.

Health care

The average German can expect to live to the age of 74. Health care is paid for by insurance plans, and Germany has many excellent hospitals.

Germans are great believers in the curing power of natural springs. They go to resorts called spas (in German, *Kurorte*) to bathe in the warm pools or drink the mineral-rich water. The most famous spa is in the southwest, at Baden-Baden. This was already famous for its public baths in the time of the ancient Romans.

Enjoy your meal!

Fresh bread and cakes in a German bakery

Germans like to eat all kinds of foods; today this includes many foreign dishes. However, traditional foods are still popular and make mouth-watering displays in shop windows. There is a wide range of local cheeses and various kinds of crusty rolls and loaves, often flavored with caraway or poppy seeds. Breads made from rye include the dark, heavy *pumpernickel* from Westphalia.

Germany is famous for its delicious pies and cakes, such as Black Forest cake. Sunday is the day to visit relatives for coffee, bringing cakes from the corner bakery.

The food served in a traditional inn, or *Gasthaus*, is filling and tasty. Soup may be made with onions, peas and beans, or peppered Hungarian-style to make *gulaschsuppe*. Favorite meats include veal and pork. These are served with potatoes or dumplings, and sometimes with spinach puree or pickled cabbage called *sauerkraut*. On the northern coasts, various fish, especially herring and eel, make popular dishes.

Schnell Imbiss — fast food!

Popular street snacks and take-out foods include french fries, or *pommes frites*. They are often served with mayonnaise or ketchup. Long sausages are served in small rolls with sharp German mustard or flavored with curry.

Super sausages

In Germany there are said to be over 1,500 varieties of sausage, from the boiled *weisswurst* to the grilled *bratwurst*! German butchers are also specialists in cold meats like salamis and smoked hams.

Eating at home

The smell of fresh coffee marks an early breakfast. This is often made up of fresh white rolls, or *brötchen*, served with cheese, jam or thin slices of ham. Sometimes there may be boiled eggs too.

The main meal of the day is often served at lunchtime. A full lunch, called *Mittagessen*, might include soup with noodles, meat with salad or vegetables and pureed apples. *Abendessen*, or supper, is lighter. A selection of cold meats and breads might be offered or perhaps an omelette with potatoes or a green salad. This might be served with apple juice, beer or wine.

Leisure and the arts

Many German children keep fit by joining local sports clubs. There is little organized athletic activity at school. Sports such as horseback riding and tennis have become popular in recent years. International German tennis stars such as Steffi Graf, Boris Becker and Michael Stich have inspired many children.

The most popular spectator sport is soccer. Teams such as Bayern Munich and Eintracht Frankfurt are among Europe's best. The national FRG team won the World Cup in 1954, 1974 and in 1990. The former GDR was also a world leader in athletics.

Hobbies and pastimes

Not all Germans are fitness fanatics! Many join clubs for less energetic hobbies, such as chess or bowling. A lot of Germans prefer to watch television, tuning in to local stations such as WDR from Cologne.

Festivals

Many people enjoy taking part in traditional festivals and fairs, such as the Rhineland carnivals or a St. Martin's Day procession. On this day, November 11, children parade through the streets with paper lanterns. In the south during Lent, carnival is called *Fasnacht* or *Fasching*. In some regions it includes parades with drums, rattles, ribbons and carved wooden masks.

There are also other regional festivals, such as target shooting, tournaments with armored knights and Munich's famous beer festival, the *Oktoberfest*.

On December 5, all over Germany, St. Nicholas arrives with small presents for the children. The main celebration is on December 24, Christmas Eve, when families gather around the Christmas tree. The idea of a decorated tree comes from Germany.

A historical festival is held each year in the beautiful old town of Dinkelsbühl.

This is a performance, in Munich, of an opera by Richard Strauss, called The Silent Woman.

Land of music

Germany has a strong musical tradition. Many of the greatest names of classical music are German, including Johann Sebastian Bach (1685–1750), George Frideric Handel (1685–1759), Ludwig van Beethoven (1770–1827) and Johannes Brahms (1833–1897). Their music is performed by famous orchestras such as the Berlin Philharmonic. The Bavarian town of Bayreuth is famous for its music festival, which stages the operas of Richard Wagner (1813–1883). Many of Wagner's operas retell the stories of ancient German myths and legends.

Folk dancers and brass bands keep up another kind of musical tradition, but young people tend to follow the latest international rock hits. Many play in bands of their own. Today Germany is also a center of opera, ballet and experimental music.

A visit to the art gallery

Art is well represented in Germany. Museums show the works of masters such as Albrecht Dürer (1471–1528) and Hans Holbein the Younger (1497–1543), the landscapes of the Dresden painter Caspar David Friedrich (1774–1840) and the bold, colorful pictures painted by the artists of the Expressionism movement after 1905.

In smaller galleries and public places, there are "art markets" and exciting exhibitions by today's artists and sculptors.

Writers and publishers

Books have played an important role in Germany. German authors were often political rebels, such as Friedrich von Schiller (1759–1805) and Heinrich Heine (1797–1856). They are still read around the world. Thomas Mann (1875–1955) and Bertolt Brecht (1898–1956) had to flee to the United States after opposing Nazi rule during the 1930s. Since World War II new German writers such as Günter Grass and Heinrich Böll have become widely read.

The traditional center of German book publishing is the city of Leipzig. However, at Frankfurt-am-Main each autumn the world's largest book fair is held. It is visited by publishers from all around the world.

Germany in history

In ancient times Germany was covered in dense forests. About 3,000 years ago this wild countryside was inhabited by people known as Celts. Their most powerful tribes lived in the Danube valley in about 800 B.C. Later the center of Celtic power moved northward and westward, to the Hunsrück and Eifel regions. The grave of a Celtic chieftain was discovered in the Black Forest in 1968. He was dressed in gold and surrounded by magnificent wealth.

German tribes

From about 500 B.C. onward, the forests between the Rhine and Danube were invaded by fierce tribes from the north and east, who spoke languages we call Germanic. These were the ancestors of today's Germans. They drove out the Celts but then began to clash with the growing power of Rome.

Between 225 and 51 B.C., the ancient Romans seized Gaul — the Celtic land lying to the south and west of Germany.

They advanced to the Rhine and the Danube. Could they now take control of the German forests? They tried, but in A.D. 9 they suffered a terrible defeat at the hands of the German tribe leader called Hermann, or Arminius.

The Roman Empire

The parts of Germany ruled by the Romans were mostly peaceful. Trade flourished and vines were planted along the warm river valleys. Towns and fortresses were built. Roman remains can still be seen at Trier, Cologne, Mainz, Augsburg and Regensburg.

However, Roman power began to weaken, and German tribes such as the Alemans, Franks, Goths and Vandals began to move south and westward. They were themselves being attacked in the east by fierce Asian tribes such as the Huns.

Germanic invaders conquered Rome in A.D. 476 and poured into Italy, France, Britain, Spain and North Africa. They set up powerful kingdoms.

This is a reconstruction of a Stone Age village from around 5000 B.C.

Germany, and its crown eventually passed to the Saxon rulers. One of these, Otto I, set up the Holy Roman Empire, which lasted from 962 to 1806. The emperor was overall ruler, but there were many regional rulers who gradually took more power for themselves. Various royal families took over the imperial crown until 1483, when the Habsburg family took it and kept it.

A changing world

Germany in the Middle Ages was a land of castles, monasteries and great cathedrals. Scholars and poets wandered from court to court. Most people worked on the land for the local lord. A new class of people became very wealthy. They were bankers, skilled craftsmen and merchants. The traders of the Hanseatic league became as rich and powerful as many rulers.

The founder of the new Europe

The Franks set up the most successful of the new Germanic kingdoms. Under the Christian ruler Charlemagne (A.D. 742-814), Frankish rule extended from the Pyrenees in the west to the Elbe River in the east. Charlemagne ruled northern Italy and in 800 was crowned emperor of Rome. His courts became centers of learning.

Catholic and Protestant

Germany became bitterly divided over religion. Protestants, led by Martin Luther (1483–1546), complained about the corruption of the Roman Catholic church and demanded that German Christians break away. Luther was supported by some rulers, but others supported the emperor, who remained Catholic. This dispute tore Germany apart. After the Thirty Years' War (1618–1648) Germany broke into no fewer than 1,800 separate states! However, during the 1700s Prussia in the Protestant northeast gradually rose to power.

The Holy Roman Empire

After Charlemagne's death, the empire was divided. The western part eventually became France. The eastern part became

United — and divided

Ruled by King Frederick the Great (1712–1786), Prussia became one of the most powerful countries in Europe. In 1806 it was invaded by France, but nine years later Prussia had its revenge, when it joined with Britain to defeat the French, led by Napoleon, at Waterloo. The Holy Roman Empire was now replaced by independent nations. However, the German people were no better off. Revolutionaries demanded reform and a united Germany.

In 1871 the German nations became a single empire. King Wilhelm I of Prussia became German emperor, or *Kaiser*.

The German Empire spread as it seized colonies in Africa. In 1914 World War I broke out. Millions were killed, and by 1918 Germany lay in ruins.

Industry and invention

During the 1800s Germany became an important industrial nation. Germany's first steam-powered train ran between Nuremberg and Fürth in 1835. German inventors had great success in science and engineering.

1851 Hermann von Helmholtz invents ophthalmoscope, used by doctors for examining the eye.

1881 Werner von Siemens builds first electric streetcar line in Berlin.

1885 Gottlieb Daimler pioneers first gas-engined motorcycle.

1885 Carl Benz produces first gas-driven automobile.

1892 Rudolf Diesel invents diesel engine.

1895 Wilhelm Röntgen discovers X rays.

The first motorcycle to run on gasoline was designed by Gottlieb Daimler.

In the 1930s young Germans were encouraged to join Nazi groups.

The rise of the Nazis

After the defeat of Germany in World War I, the *Kaiser*, Wilhelm II, went into exile in the Netherlands. Germany became a republic. Communists attempted to take control, but failed. Unfortunately, during the 1920s and 1930s there was great hardship, with many people out of work. Money became worth so little that a suitcase full of bank notes was needed to buy even a loaf of bread.

In 1933 Adolf Hitler, leader of the Nazi (National Socialist German Workers') party, became German chancellor. The Nazis beat up, imprisoned or murdered anyone who disagreed with them. In 1939 Hitler led his country into World War II against the Allies, which included France, Britain, the Soviet Union and, from 1941, the United States. However, by 1945 Germany was utterly destroyed. As the Allies advanced into German territory, they were horrified to find death camps where the Nazis had murdered over six million Jews.

Germany divided

Germany was now freed from Nazi rule, but it was split into two halves. The United States, who supported the FRG, and the Soviet Union, who controlled the GDR, had become enemies. Families were divided. Large armies faced each other across the barbed wire of the frontier.

On both sides Germans set about rebuilding their country. The FRG was so successful that it was said an "economic miracle" had taken place.

In the late 1980s the Soviet Union began to break up. On November 10, 1989, the hated Berlin Wall was demolished. Germany was united again.

The Berlin Wall before it was pulled down

Facing the future

These SPD supporters are at a rally in the GDR, before Germany was united.

During a general election, various political parties put forward their plans for the future of Germany. The CDU and CSU are conservative. The SPD has a social democratic platform. These parties have governed Germany since World War II, sometimes joining together in a coalition with the liberal FDP.

In the 1950s the West German Communist party (KPD) was banned from the FRG. In the 1960s many young people turned toward socialist groups, which often used violence to try and bring change. In the 1980s the people of the FRG became very conscious of environmental problems, and the Green party became important in politics. Some German parties have tried to bring back the politics of the Nazi period. They have few members, but there are fears that new right-wing parties such as the Republicans may be more successful.

Foreign workers

In the 1950s *Gastarbeiter*, or foreign workers, were encouraged to come to the FRG but they have often been poorly treated. Recently, there have also been many refugees from Eastern European and African countries. Unemployment is increasing, and foreigners have been attacked by German racists. Many Germans have protested against these attacks and demanded justice for all foreigners who live in Germany.

Making one country

The early 1990s are difficult times for Germany as the problems of joining east and west become clearer. People in the GDR were used to state control of industry, and there was no unemployment. Some GDR firms were inefficient and did not produce goods to a standard expected in the west. East German firms that were once state-owned are now being bought up by private companies. Many East Germans feel that they are not getting a fair deal. Many West Germans are afraid of losing their jobs to people from East Germany.

East Germans were able to see many more goods after uniting with the FRG, but did not often have the money to buy them.

These young people are protesting against nuclear power.

Young Germans have also protested against pollution of the environment and against the use of nuclear power to generate electricity.

Many of Germany's political debates are ones that are taking place across Europe. Germany was one of the founders of the European Community, and many Germans wish to see a united Europe. However, some are worried about plans to replace the German mark with a single European currency.

One thing is certain. Most young people in Germany wish to grow up in a peaceful, healthy and fairer world.

Fact file

Government

Germany is a democracy, which means that the people elect the rulers. The German head of state is called the president and is elected every five years. The leader of the government is called the chancellor. The German parliament is known as the Federal Assembly, or *Bundestag*, and elections to it take place every four years. The *Länder* have their own regional governments but send delegates to the Federal Council, or *Bundesrat*.

Flag

The German flag, adopted by the FRG in 1949, was first flown in the 1800s. Its colors of black, red and gold were worn by soldiers during the wars against Napoléon.

National anthem

The German national anthem is sung to an internationally known tune composed by Franz Joseph Haydn in 1797. It is called "*Einigkeit und Recht und Freiheit,*" or "Unity and Right and Freedom."

Religion

Most Germans are Christians. Traditionally, the north and east are Protestant, while the south and west are mostly Roman Catholic. There are now a growing number of Muslims, too (1.5 million in 1987).

Money

The German unit of currency is the *Deutsche Mark* (DM). It is divided into 100 *Pfennig* (pf). The ECU, or European Currency Unit, is sometimes used for business with other countries.

Education

Nearly all schools are state owned. Education is organized by the government of each *Land*. All children must go to school for at least nine years starting from the age of 6. Secondary school begins at 11. There are several kinds of secondary school. In some *Länder* all children go to comprehensive schools, or *Gesamtschulen*. In others, children may go to *Hauptschulen* or *Realschulen*, which prepare children for learning a trade and for technical college courses. Pupils begin at the technical colleges when they are 15 or 16. Children who go to *Gymnasien*, or grammar schools, may stay until they are over 20 years old. The final school certificate, or *Abitur*, is taken in all subjects. Most pupils who pass all subjects have the right to go to a university.

Newspapers and television

Newspapers, comics and magazines of all kinds are published right across Germany. Many have a strong regional flavor. There are two national and one regional television channels, as well as satellite communications and cable.

Some famous people

Walther von der Vogelweide (1170–1230) was a poet of the Middle Ages

Johannes Gutenberg (1400–1468) pioneered printing

Albrecht Dürer (1471–1528) was an artist

Martin Luther (1483–1546) was a Protestant religious reformer

Johann Kepler (1571–1630) was an astronomer

Gottfried Leibniz (1646--1716) was a philosopher and mathematician

Johann Sebastian Bach (1685–1750) was a musical composer

Frederick II (the Great, 1712–1786) was king of Prussia

Johann Wolfgang von Goethe (1749–1832) was a poet, playwright and scientist

Friedrich von Schiller (1759–1805) was a poet, playwright and historian

Ludwig van Beethoven (1770–1827) was a musical composer

Georg Simon Ohm (1787–1854) worked out laws of electricity

Otto von Bismarck (1815–1898) was a statesman

Karl Marx (1818–1883) was a Communist and political writer

Wilhelm Röntgen (1845–1923) discovered X rays

Albert Einstein (1879–1955) was a mathematician and physicist

Adolf Hitler (1889–1945) was a Nazi dictator

Marlene Dietrich (1901–1992) was an international movie star

Some key events in history

A.D. **9**: Romans defeated by Arminius (Hermann)

742: Charlemagne was born

1076: Henry IV clashed with the pope

1190: Death of Frederick I, known as Barbarossa, the greatest of medieval emperors

1241: North German merchants grouped together, forerunners of the Hanseatic league

1309: Marienburg Castle in Poland became the headquarters of the Teutonic knights

1517: Martin Luther made public his Protestant beliefs

1618: Start of the Thirty Years' War

1712: Birth of Frederick the Great, king of Prussia

1806: Prussia defeated by France at Jena

1871: William I of Prussia became emperor of a united Germany

1884: Start of German Empire in Africa

1914: Outbreak of World War I

1918: Germany defeated

1919: Founding of the Weimar Republic

1933: Adolf Hitler became chancellor

1935: Nazi laws passed against Jews

1939: Outbreak of World War II

1941: United States enters war

1945: Germany defeated

1949: Germany divided into GDR and FRG

1957: FRG cofounder of European Economic Community, now European Community

1961-89: Berlin divided by wall

1990: GDR joins FRG: Germany reunites

Index